STAR WARS
ROGUE ONE ™
ULTIMATE STICKER ENCYCLOPEDIA

HOW TO USE THIS BOOK

Read the captions, then find the sticker that best fits the space. (Hint: check the bold sticker labels for clues!)

There are lots of extra stickers for creating your own scenes throughout the book.

Learn more about the Rogue One team, the vehicles, and the action from across the *Star Wars* galaxy.

Whiskers of
Iakaru race

Protective
headgear

Blaster
rifle

Marine
fatigues

BISTAN AND PAO

Penguin
Random
House

Written and edited by Emma Grange and Shari Last
Designed by Chris Gould and Owen Bennett
Consultant Jason Fry

For Lucasfilm
Editor Samantha Holland
Image Unit Newell Todd, Gabrielle Levenson,
Erik Sanchez, Bryce Pinkos, and Tim Mapp
Story Group Pablo Hidalgo, Leland Chee, and Matt Martin
Creative Director of Publishing Michael Siglain

First American Edition, 2016
Published in the United States by DK Publishing
345 Hudson Street, New York, NY 10014

Page design copyright © 2016 Dorling Kindersley Limited
DK, a division of Penguin Random House LLC

16 17 18 19 20 10 9 8 7 6 5 4 3 2 1
001–280849–December/2016

© & TM 2016 LUCASFILM LTD.

A catalog record for this book is available from the Library of Congress.

ISBN: 978-1-4654-5266-5

DK books are available at special discounts when purchased in bulk for sales promotions, premiums, fund-raising, or educational use. For details, contact: DK Publishing Special Markets, 345 Hudson Street, New York, New York 10014
SpecialSales@dk.com

Printed and bound in China

A WORLD OF IDEAS:
SEE ALL THERE IS TO KNOW

www.dk.com
www.starwars.com

THE EMPIRE

EMPEROR PALPATINE'S MILITARY FORCES are on the march, seizing control of many planets and brutally clamping down on those opposed to his rule. A few brave senators and bands of rebels still battle the Empire, but Imperial scientists are preparing a secret weapon—the Death Star—that will bring an end to opposition!

THE *DEVASTATOR*
Darth Vader's flagship ferries the Emperor's apprentice on missions across the galaxy, and carries battle-hardened stormtroopers loyal to Vader.

KRENNIC'S SHUTTLE
This bat-winged *Delta*-class command shuttle transports Krennic on Imperial missions. Its wings descend in flight and fold up for landing.

White uniform worn as part of Advanced Weapons Research for the Imperial Military

Imperial insignia denotes rank of director

Polished belt clasp contains data storage

ORSON KRENNIC
Krennic has staked his reputation on completing the Death Star, and will stop at nothing to achieve that goal.

WEAPONS MASTER
Imperial Director of Weapons Research Krennic possesses a dangerous combination of intelligence, determination, and ruthlessness. He is obsessed with proving himself to Emperor Palpatine.

SERVANTS OF THE EMPIRE

KRENNIC'S GUARDS
Some high ranking officers, including Krennic, have their own enforcers to ensure work on the Death Star continues on time.

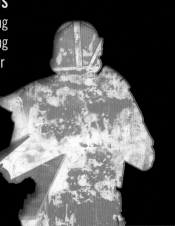

IMPERIAL GUARDS
The loyal Imperial Guards carry pikes that can be used to defend the Emperor and servants such as Darth Vader.

DARTH VADER
The Emperor's terrifying enforcer, Vader has been assigned to keep Krennic on schedule.

THE DEATH STAR
The Empire's monstrous weapon is the size of a small moon. But this massive space station has a hidden flaw in its construction.

The Death Star is 120km (75 miles) in diameter

Outer hull made from quadanium steel

FACT FILE

The Emperor maintains control of his Empire from the planet Coruscant. He often sends instructions to Vader via hologram.

Housing for focusing lens

UNDER CONSTRUCTION
When complete, the Death Star will have the power to destroy entire planets with one blast from its superlaser. It is Krennic's job to make it operational.

ROGUE ONE

THE EMPIRE IS READY to conduct the biggest weapons test in its history. Desperate to stop this threat, an unlikely band of warriors with a broad range of skills assembles, united by one goal—discover what the Empire's weapon is and find a way to destroy it.

A BAND OF ROGUES
Rebels, mercenaries, ex-Imperials, and a droid make up the team that becomes known as Rogue One.

JYN ERSO
Hot-tempered Jyn is assigned to the mission to stop the Empire. Initially reluctant, she becomes the team's leader.

CASSIAN ANDOR
Cassian Andor is a trusted member of the rebel forces. He puts his intelligence skills to good use.

K-2SO
This Imperial enforcer droid was reprogrammed when he crossed enemy lines. K-2SO is now loyal to the rebels.

CHIRRUT ÎMWE
A blind warrior-monk and a disciplined fighter, Chirrut is attuned to the mystical energy known as the Force.

BAZE MALBUS
Well-armed Baze is always battle-ready. He has his own scores to settle with the Empire.

BODHI ROOK
Originally an Imperial pilot, Bodhi defects to joins the rebels. He brings hacking and communications expertise to the team.

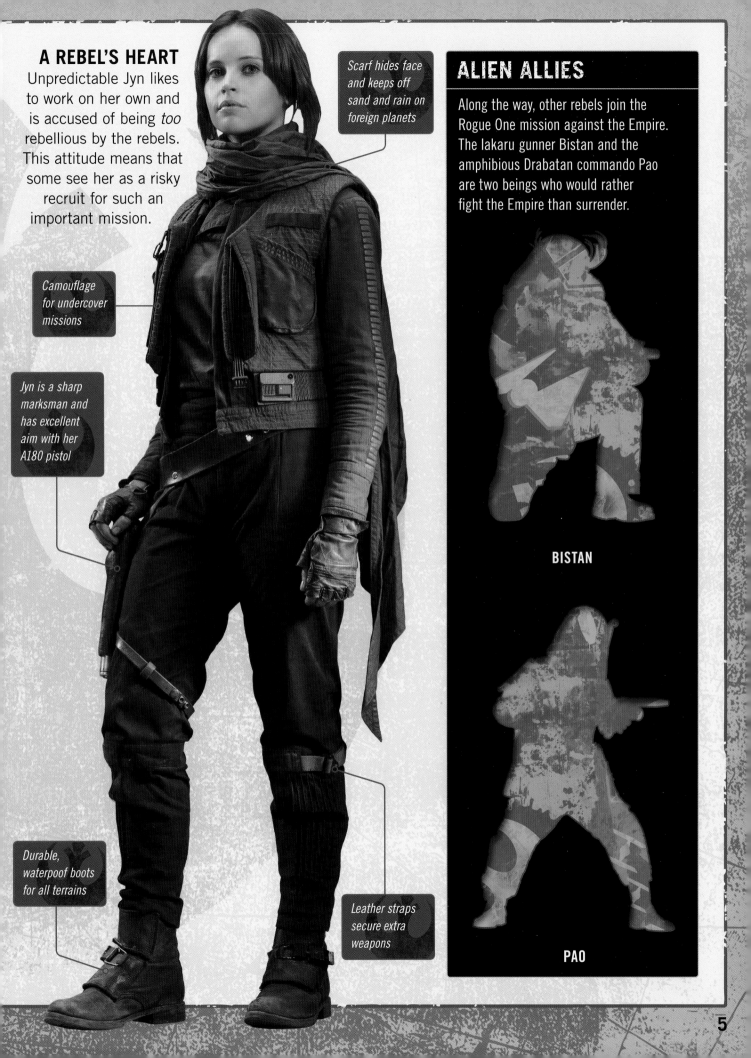

A REBEL'S HEART

Unpredictable Jyn likes to work on her own and is accused of being *too* rebellious by the rebels. This attitude means that some see her as a risky recruit for such an important mission.

Scarf hides face and keeps off sand and rain on foreign planets

Camouflage for undercover missions

Jyn is a sharp marksman and has excellent aim with her A180 pistol

Durable, waterpoof boots for all terrains

Leather straps secure extra weapons

ALIEN ALLIES

Along the way, other rebels join the Rogue One mission against the Empire. The Iakaru gunner Bistan and the amphibious Drabatan commando Pao are two beings who would rather fight the Empire than surrender.

BISTAN

PAO

REBEL HQ

THE RESISTANCE to the Empire is shadowed by personal disagreements. Some rebel leaders are determined to fight, while others believe political negotiations could succeed. But all understand they must stop the Empire's superweapon—and they have new hope in Jyn Erso.

Ceremonial silver chain

White robes of office, symbol of peace

A FATHER'S CALL
The rebel leaders need Jyn to find her father, Galen Erso—the scientist warning them about the Empire's new weapon.

YAVIN BASE
The rebels' temple headquarters is hidden away from the Empire on Yavin 4—a moon orbiting a gas giant in the Outer Rim.

MON MOTHMA
Senator Mon Mothma led the secret opposition to the Emperor's rise. Now the top-ranking rebel leader, it's her decision to trust Jyn with her mission.

TACTFUL LEADER
As a respected former member of the Senate—the galactic government now weakened by Emperor Palpatine—Mon Mothma understands it's important to listen to all points of view.

ADMIRAL RADDUS

Mon Calamari officer Raddus was one of the earliest opponents of the Empire and holds a command in the rebel navy. The veteran is dedicated to the rebel cause.

Blue rebel naval uniform

GENERAL DRAVEN

Gruff General Draven prefers action to talking. Suspicious of Jyn at first, he takes steps to ensure her mission will succeed if she falters.

GENERAL DODONNA

A skilled tactician, Jan Dodonna is known for his ability to size up a situation and find a critical weak point in an enemy's battle plan.

Waterproof skin indigenous to Mon Calamari race and their ocean world

GENERAL MERRICK

Flying as Blue Leader, Merrick is protective of the brave U-wing pilots under his command and watches out for their interests in strategy talks.

Belt-affixed secure datapad contains fleet information

FACT FILE

After the Empire brought war to their homeworld, the Mon Calamari armed the rebels by building massive star cruisers for their fleet.

WHICH SIDE?

WITH THE EMPIRE growing in power, it is not always easy to know who to trust, or who is working for whom. Some beings working for the Empire are secretly aiding the rebels, while others have made the brave choice to defy the Empire publicly.

KEEPING SECRETS
Cassian is committed to the rebels, but has his own secret mission to accomplish, which brings him into conflict with Jyn. Can he be trusted?

SAW GERRERA
A veteran resistance fighter, Saw now believes that violence is the only way to stop the Empire. He leads his own band of fighters on the planet Jedha.

PLAYING SIDES
Jyn is warned that her mission might change her—but this Imperial outfit is a disguise, not a sign that she has switched sides!

FACT FILE
The rebel leaders have turned their backs on Saw and his team of rebel fighters, worried that his violent methods will undermine support for their cause.

PILOT IN PERIL
Bodhi joined the Empire because he wanted to fly. He's happy to leave his past behind, but remains anxious about the consequences of this choice.

TOGNATHIAN SOLDIERS
Warrior pilots Edrio and Benthic fly with Saw Gerrera's squadron, the Cavern Angels. They wear breathing apparatuses that allow them to breathe in different atmospheres.

GALEN ERSO

Brilliant scientist Galen Erso hoped to escape the Empire by fleeing to his farm on Lah'mu, but Imperials track him down.

Imperial ranking for scientists

Imperial code cylinder

Tunic worn in days working for the Empire on Coruscant

ERSO FAMILY

Galen would do anything to protect his wife Lyra and his daughter, Jyn. When Krennic threatens them, Galen returns with Krennic to work on the Death Star.

GALEN ERSO'S DAUGHTER

The Rebel Council counts resisting arrest, forgery, and assault amongst Jyn's crimes. But they give her a chance to do good for their cause.

A SECRET MESSAGE

At one point, Galen Erso and Orson Krennic were friends. However, when Galen learned that his scientific work for the Empire was being used to create a horrifying weapon, he fled. Forced to return and work on the Death Star, Galen risks his life by contacting the rebels to warn them about the battle station.

PLANETS

THE PLANET-DESTROYING Death Star superlaser poses a terrible danger to the galaxy's worlds. With resistance to Imperial rule threatening to explode into open war, both the Empire and the rebels have sought out planets to use as secret bases in the coming struggle.

SCARIF
Tropical Scarif looks idyllic, but is actually an Imperial military stronghold, heavily defended to protect the construction site of the Emperor's dreaded Death Star.

LAH'MU
A simple planet, Lah'mu is a sanctuary for Galen Erso's family after they flee the Empire. But their peace does not last.

Polarized lenses reduce glare during battle

Plastoid armor can't withstand direct laser hits

E-11 blaster rifle is standard Imperial issue

YAVIN 4
The vast jungle covering the surface of Yavin offers camouflage for the rebels, whose base is built inside an ancient Massassi temple.

FACT FILE
Kyber crystals collected on Jedha are transported under enormous security to the Death Star, where they're key elements of the superlaser.

IMPERIAL BASE
Scarif is heavily defended by troops, such as stormtroopers, as well as deflector shields and weapons. This makes it seem impenetrable to the rebels.

EADU

Rainy Eadu is an unwelcoming planet. This makes it the perfect location for Krennic to hide his scientists while they work on the Death Star.

JEDHA

An ancient world, dusty Jedha is a place of holy pilgrimage, but is now occupied by Imperial troops.

KRENNIC'S VISION

The Empire believes that fear of the Death Star's planet-destroying power will remove all opposition to the Empire across the whole galaxy—a vision Krennic seeks to make a reality.

JEDHA INHABITANTS

Jedha is both a holy site—home to an ancient temple—and a busy Imperial territory. As such it attracts a range of travelers—including pilgrims and mercenaries such as Weeteef Cyu-Bee and Moroff.

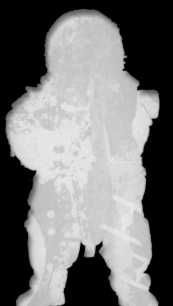

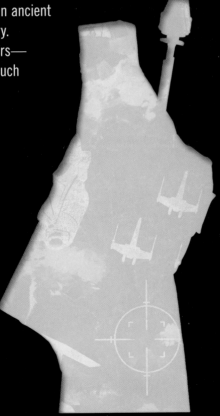

WEETEEF CYU-BEE   **HOLY CITY PILGRIM**   **MOROFF**

UNLIKELY ALLIANCES

THE EMPIRE'S RULE has driven wedges between old friends while uniting strangers out of necessity. Many alliances have been formed between people who seem to have nothing in common, but who are fighting for the same goal—the downfall of the Empire.

JYN AND CASSIAN

When they first meet, Cassian keeps secrets from Jyn, causing distrust between them. Working together helps Jyn realize that Cassian is a true friend.

FACT FILE

From the first alliance of Jyn, Cassian, and K-2SO, the Rogue One team grows to recruit Baze, Chirrut, and Bodhi.

Jyn must learn to work with the rebel leadership, despite her lack of patience.

Cassian must decide whether to trust Jyn in their mission against the Empire.

Bodhi must find courage to turn against the Empire.

Baze must decide how far he will go to fight for freedom.

Chirrut relies on his faith to stay calm when in danger.

A MOTLEY CREW

This unlikely team would not have been the rebel leaders' first choice for the vital mission to steal the Death Star plans. However, they prove themselves by sticking together to the end, drawing on each other's strengths in time of need.

REBEL FACTIONS
Some rebels believe peace can be found through negotiations, while others think that's impossible. They must work hard to put their differences aside.

DRAVEN'S DOUBTS
General Draven finds it hard to trust Jyn at first. But after she proves herself to him, he comes to her team's aid when they're in danger on Scarif.

BAZE AND CHIRRUT
Baze and Chirrut used to work together. A falling out saw them go their separate ways, before renewing their friendship many years later.

FATHER FIGURE
Saw Gerrera rescued Jyn from death troopers on Lah'mu and taught her how to fight the Empire. But he also taught her what she isn't willing to do in the struggle for freedom.

FORMER COMRADES
Once friends, Krennic and Galen became adversaries after Galen realized the extent of the Empire's evil ways.

DIVIDED LOYALTIES
Krennic demands absolute loyalty to the Empire. When Galen tries to flee Imperial service, his former friend forces him to return.

Galen sees peace through terror as no peace at all.

Krennic thinks fear of the Death Star will ensure galactic peace.

Death troopers watch and wait for Krennic's orders.

ON THE DEATH STAR

MAIN CONSTRUCTION BEGAN on the Death Star many years ago, but the superweapon has proved difficult to turn into reality. At the battle station's core is a superlaser focused by kyber crystals mined across the galaxy. This massive operation is a tightly kept secret—until a rogue scientist alerts the rebels to its existence.

DEATH STAR DIRECTOR
Krennic is not the only one in charge of the Death Star project, but he is using his position of power to gain favor with the Emperor as much as possible.

A LOOMING THREAT
The Death Star is nearing completion. The final work is taking place above the planet Scarif, but Krennic seeks a target on which to test the battle station's destructive potential.

IMPERIAL SCIENTISTS

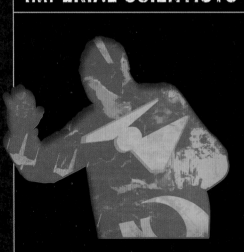

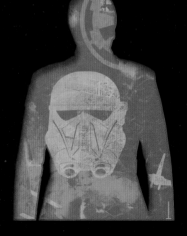

SCIENTIST FEYN VANN
Like Erso, many of the scientists working on the Death Star have been chosen for their intelligence and forced to do the Empire's bidding.

IMPERIAL TRAITOR
Galen Erso has risked his life to warn the rebels of the Death Star's existence and to give them a chance to find its hidden weakness.

CONTROL ROOM
The Death Star's operations are overseen from a control room that looks out over the vast expanse of space—with the battle station's current target front and center.

FACT FILE

The Death Star employs more than 300,000 crew, including scientists, technicians, naval personnel, stormtroopers, and droids.

DEATH STAR TROOPER

The Death Star is defended by more than its superlaser. Black-clad Death Star troopers guard against rebel infiltration attempts.

A FATAL FLAW

Erso knows the Death Star is not as invulnerable as the Empire believes. A weak spot lies hidden deep within its plans.

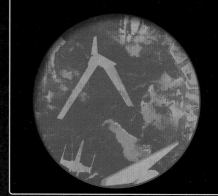

Armored helmet contains life support and breathing mask

Commands issued via a voice box

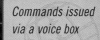

Control panel

DEATH STAR GUNNER

Death Star gunners control the battle station's surface turbolasers and the superlaser operating stations.

OBEYING ORDERS

Though Darth Vader carries out his Emperor's wishes, he does not believe the Death Star to be worthy of much attention.

RULE OF FEAR

The Emperor's emissary, Darth Vader, is a Sith Lord strong in the powerful Force. His terrifying appearance ensures those around him obey his commands— or face terrible consequences.

DEATH STAR CONTROL ROOM

The control room on board the Death Star is where its powerful planet-obliterating superlaser can be prepared and fired. From here, Krennic must decide the fate of the planet Jedha, and others like it.

DROIDS

THE GALAXY DEPENDS ON droids to do jobs that are too dangerous or dull for living beings. Both Imperials and rebels use mechanical minions for purposes ranging from espionage and navigation, to providing power and medical assistance.

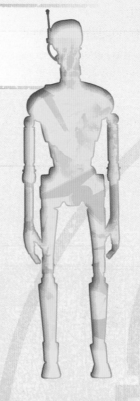

ASTROMECHS

Astromech droids help their masters by fixing systems on starships. These small, sturdy droids also assist starfighter pilots by calculating courses in space.

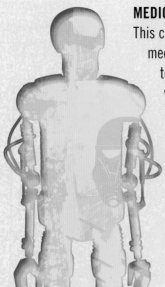

MEDICAL DROID
This customized 2-1B medical droid tends to Saw Gerrera, who requires constant medical attention, in his caves on the planet Jedha.

HOMESTEAD DROID
Homestead droids often do menial tasks for their owners, and are programmed to remain loyal. This one works for the Erso family on Lah'mu.

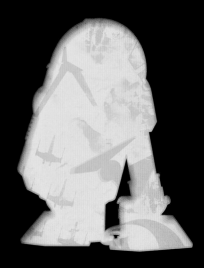

IMPERIAL ASTROMECH: C2-B5

COMMUNICATIONS DROID
Communications droids are often humanoid in shape. They carry messages and assist their masters during negotiations.

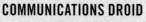

PROTOCOL DROID
On the Death Star, protocol droids with insectoid heads, such as this one, carry out Imperial commands.

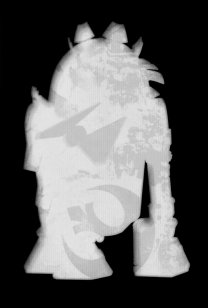

REBEL ASTROMECH: R2-BHD

GNK DROID
GNK power droids can be found on the rebel base on Yavin 4. These droids are simple but useful, powering up vehicles in the rebels' hangar.

MOUSE DROID
MSE-6 "mouse" droids work on the Death Star and have a very important job—cleaning the many floors on the battle station!

R3-S1
This rebel astromech droid has a clear dome that reveals its interior parts. Droids like this are known for their speedy processing skills.

REPROGRAMMED ENFORCER DROID
Having been reprogrammed, K-2SO is loyal to the rebellion and its goals. However, K-2SO still looks like an intimidating Imperial enforcer droid—which is useful for undercover rebel missions!

Photoreceptors, auditory sensors, and vocabulator encased in head unit

Olfactory sensor for smell

Imperial symbol on shoulder

Long armspan is a valuable asset

Strengthened knee joint

Strong hands capable of grabbing and punching

Long legs contribute to K-2SO's height of 2.2m (7'1").

Wide, flat foot provides surface area to support K-2SO's weight, even on sandy surfaces

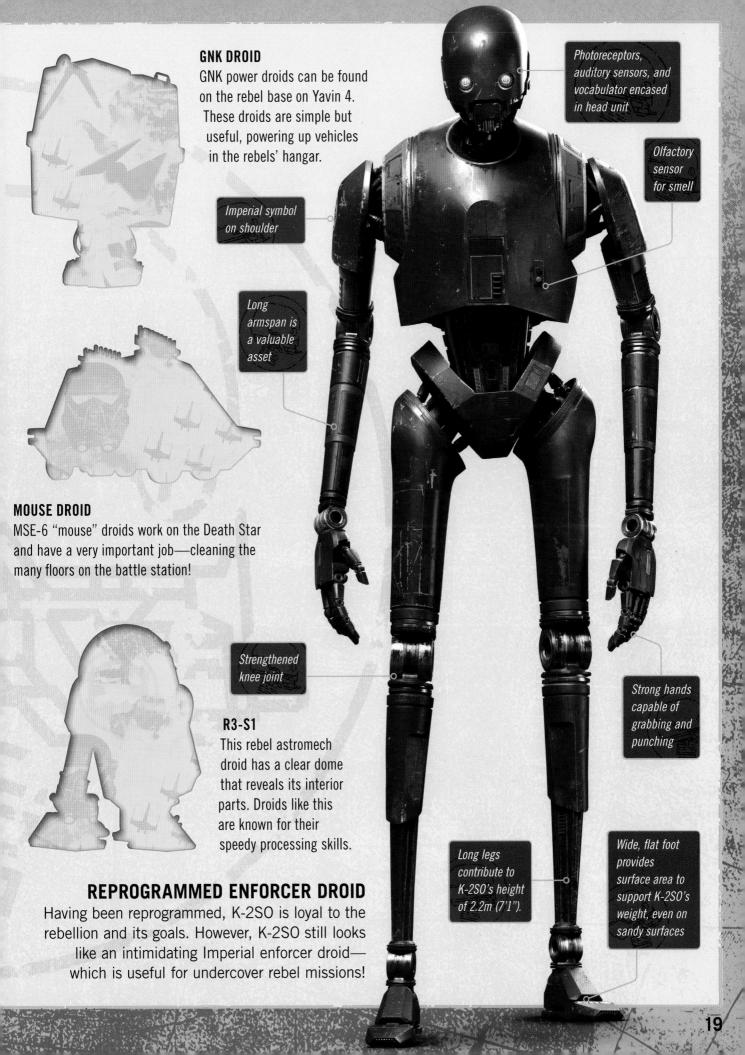

IMPERIAL TROOPS

THE EMPIRE KEEPS CONTROL of the galaxy's planets by sending in armored soldiers to destroy enemies on the battlefield and maintain steely law and order. Stormtroopers and other elite units are trained to be deadly in combat and utterly loyal to superiors' commands.

Flexible pauldron denotes rank

Additional weaponry, such as grenades, clipped onto armor

GUARD DUTY
The Empire's secret base on Scarif is heavily guarded by both Imperial ground personnel and stormtroopers.

TANK COMMANDER
Tank troopers patrol Jedha from Imperial tanks and are protected by the vehicle's thick armor casing. The commander's post on top of the vehicle offers excellent visibility.

The death trooper's SE-14 pistol can be disassembled

ELITE SOLDIERS
Clad entirely in black armor, death troopers carry specialized weapons and technology. Enemies of the Empire fear them for their combat skills and brutality.

TROOP VARIANTS

  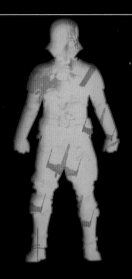 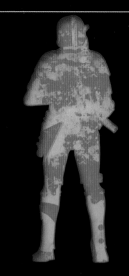

STORMTROOPER
Fearsome stormtroopers, in their all-white armor, are a familiar sight on rebellious planets.

SHORETROOPER
Shoretroopers patrol the Empire's secret Scarif base, wearing lightweight armor colored for camouflage.

TANK TROOPER
On the streets of Jedha, tank troopers wear light leg armor so they can get in and out of their tanks quickly.

DEATH TROOPER
Elite soldiers assigned to high ranking officials, these ruthless troopers serve as bodyguards and enforcers.

FACT FILE
The shoretroopers' flexible attire allows for freedom of movement when in battle on Scarif's sand dunes.

Shoretrooper captain wears red armband

HEAVY ARMOR
Stormtrooper armor is bulky and confining, as troops on Jedha discover when facing the precise attacks of Chirrut Îmwe.

FALL OUT
At the first sign of rebel activity, Imperial forces scramble to mount a defense, with all troops rushing to respond to the alarm.

HOW TO BE A REBEL

REBELS KNOW THAT their missions will lead them into many dangerous situations. Each rebel must be prepared to go undercover, face capture, engage in battle, and even risk his or her own safety. To succeed, rebels must use their skills to overcome the obstacles they face.

UNDERCOVER
Jyn and Cassian don Imperial uniforms to deceive their enemies. They must act with confidence to avoid being discovered.

SLICING SKILLS
Bodhi uses his knowledge of the Empire and his hacking skills—known as slicing—to infiltrate Imperial computer systems.

STEALTH
This mining craft usually carries kyber crystals to the Scarif base. The rebels steal it and use it to sneak behind enemy lines.

Tough, amphibious skin of Drabatan species

Pao uses the powerful battle cry "Sa'kalla" in combat

Spare ammo worn strapped to arm

Tibanna-jacked boiler rifle

KEEPING CALM

To triumph in the face of overwhelming odds, Jyn and her fellow rebels, such as Pao, must be able to remain cool under fire and during the perils of battle.

INITIATIVE
Jyn uses her initiative to gather intelligence. She finds her old mentor Saw, who gives her information vital to the mission ahead.

Built-in comlink

Protective vest with added utility pockets

LEADERSHIP
Jyn proves her leadership skills when she convinces her fellow rebels about the importance of their mission.

LOYALTY
Loyalty keeps a team from fragmenting. Baze and Chirrut show great loyalty, helping each other and Jyn instead of running from danger.

BRAVERY
A true rebel must be brave. Though her life is in danger, Jyn swears she will complete her mission at all costs.

A280-CFE blaster rifle

FACT FILE
The Rogue One team learns that the Death Star plans are held in a vault on the planet Scarif. To destroy the Death Star, they must try to steal them.

REBEL HERO
Cassian displays all the qualities needed to be a rebel hero. He's skilled in battle, but he's also brave and loyal—qualities that help him win victories over evil.

EQUIPPED FOR BATTLE

IT TAKES MORE THAN intensive training and careful planning to get ready for battle. The rebels must choose their weapons, armor, and equipment with care. Different battles require different tools depending on the environment and the nature of the mission.

CASSIAN'S QUADNOCULARS
Cassian relies on these compact, well-worn quadnoculars to track incoming attackers.

JYN'S GUN
Jyn is an expert shot with her compact, lightweight weapon—thanks to years of weapons training with Saw Gerrera.

> Chestplate has seen many battles

FACT FILE
Many rebel weapons are salvaged from the Empire and upgraded. Such scavenged arms are big business on the galaxy's black market.

> Cylinder uses gas compression to fire quickly

> Ammo pouches ensure Baze never runs out

> Heavy repeating blaster requires strength to operate

BAZE'S REPEATING BLASTER
This powerful, belt-fed weapon can fire at incredible speed, thanks to a compressed-gas cylinder worn on Baze's back.

> Belt automatically feeds ammo into gun

ALL GUNS BLAZING
Baze is rarely seen without his customized repeating blaster. He is easy to spot on the battlefield— charging his way past the enemy.

PERFECT AIM

Chirrut is a perceptive warrior. His heightened senses help him to sense the battle around him and choose which weapon to deploy.

Finely balanced weapon requires lots of skill

Ornate gold details

Comlink vital for keeping Chirrut informed

CHIRRUT'S BOWCASTER

Not only is Chirrut's bowcaster more accurate and powerful than most blasters, it folds up for ease of transport and can be slung over one shoulder.

Leather straps for carrying bowcaster on back

CHIRRUT'S STAFF

Chirrut's staff appears to be merely a blind man's walking stick, but is a deadly weapon in his hands.

Monk's robes

READY FOR ANYTHING

PREPARED CASSIAN

Cassian wears warm gear to travel to cold Jedha. Uncertain what the Rogue One team will encounter, he fills his backpack with potentially useful gear.

UNDERCOVER JYN

For a covert mission to locate her father on Eadu, Jyn wears a plain cloak to blend in while carrying her trusty blaster.

REBEL FLEET

THE REBELS OF YAVIN 4 have assembled a small but skilled group to oppose the Empire. From their base in the galaxy's Outer Rim, they have gathered warships and starfighters for space battles and trained marines for missions that require ground combat against Imperial forces.

Y-WING
A slow but sturdy older model of starfighter, the Y-wing is best used for bombing missions. It can absorb considerable punishment.

U-WING
The UT-60D gunship is often used as a troop transport by the rebels. Tough but maneuverable, U-wings swoop in and out of danger zones to deliver soldiers into battle.

X-WING
Fast and durable, X-wing starfighters boast multiple cannons. Their famous wings form an "x"-shape when in attack formation.

Combat helmet

Camouflage fatigues

Utility pocket holds spare ammunition

Standard rebel issue BlasTech A-280 blaster rifle has high accuracy and range

STEADY SEFLA
Confident Lieutenant Sefla leads a platoon in the rebel SpecForces—a highly skilled branch of the rebel marines. Sefla firmly believes in making every action count.

FACT FILE
Behind the scenes, the troops on the ground are commanded by Sefla and the navy by Admiral Raddus.

REBEL FORCES

U-WING PILOTS
U-wing pilots need to have steely resolve and a keen focus to land their U-wings safely amid the chaos of a combat zone.

X-WING AND Y-WING PILOTS
Both X-wing and Y-wing pilots wear similar flight uniforms. Flying these starfighters requires quick reflexes and is a true test of a pilot's ability.

REBEL MARINES
SpecForces commandos such as Kappehl and Basteren are brave and resilient. They work in small groups, often with small odds of success.

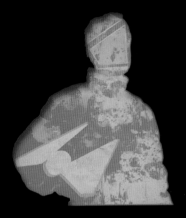

HEFF TOBBER

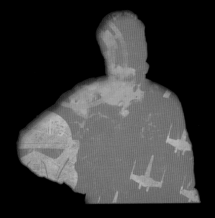

HARB BINLI

PRIVATE KAPPEHL

"BLUE FOUR"

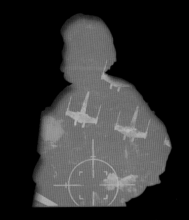

ZAL DINNES

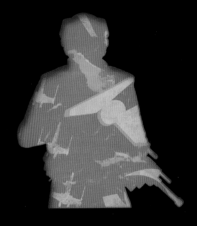

PRIVATE BASTEREN

FLIGHT HELMETS

X-wing pilots, U-wing pilots, and Y-wing pilots all wear uniquely decorated helmets—which the pilots often customize themselves.

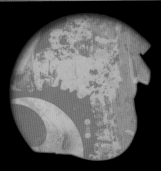

HELMET 1

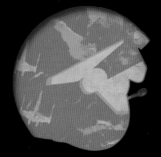

HELMET 2

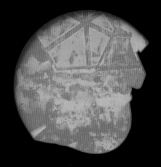

HELMET 3

27

IMPERIAL MIGHT

THE EMPIRE is a war machine unlike anything in galactic history. Armored vehicles support its armies, while fleets of warships and starfighter squadrons control space. From its Scarif secret base to the Jedha occupation, the Empire rules through intimidating displays of military might.

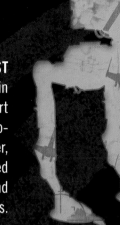

AT-ST
The All Terrain Scout Transport (AT-ST) is a two-legged walker, most often used for scouting and patrol missions.

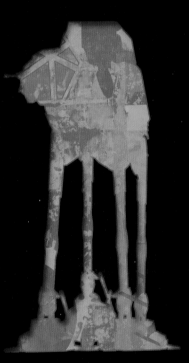

IMPERIAL TANK
The armored TX-225 assault tank has powerful engines for maneuverability in tight spaces such as Jedha's streets.

AT-ACT
The All Terrain Armored Cargo Transport (AT-ACT) is the Empire's largest walker. Often seen at construction sites, its orange cargo bed is designed to carry heavy building materials or munitions.

IMPERIAL CREW

The Empire picks only the very best to fill the ranks of its Starfighter Corps. Pilots assigned to TIEs train ceaselessly to prepare for deep-space missions and attacks on ground targets, and black-clad landing-crew members take pride in their ability to guide Imperial fighters back down to safety.

TIE FIGHTER PILOT   **LANDING CREW**

ON THE OFFENSIVE

AT-ACTs transport cargo, but boast powerful weapons. When Yavin 4's rebels attack Scarif's Imperial base, the AT-ACTs use their laser cannons to fire on the marines.

TIE FIGHTER

Light armor and powerful engines make TIE fighters fast and nimble. They lack shields, forcing pilots to survive through skill and nerve.

TIE STRIKER

Streamlined hulls make TIE strikers more maneuverable in planetary atmospheres.

STRIKING FEAR

TIE strikers can fly in space, but are specifically designed for flight in the atmosphere of a planet, where they are faster than regular TIEs. They are a feared part of the Imperial fleet.

Wing brace

Twin ion engines similar to those in TIE fighters

Access hatch located at rear of vehicle

Wide surface area for solar energy collection

Main central viewport

Laser weapons sit under main body

DEADLY BATTLES

THE ROGUE ONE TEAM'S MISSION to learn about the Death Star takes them all across the galaxy, from one dangerous situation to another. On each planet that they visit, they encounter armed Imperials and the threat of battle—culminating on the planet Scarif. Will they overcome the odds against them?

SCARIF BEACH ASSAULT
To retrieve the Death Star plans, the rebels must first battle the troopers guarding the land and sea of Scarif.

AT-ACT ATTACK
The Empire might be caught by surprise when the rebels attack their base on Scarif, but they are equipped to respond—with troops and vehicles.

SCARIF SKY BATTLE
From his rebel command ship, Admiral Raddus commands the rebel fleet in space battles—such as the one that takes place above Scarif.

EXPLOSIVE EXIT

The mining craft stolen by the rebels to sneak past the Empire meets an unfortunate end on Scarif when it is blown up by an Imperial grenade.

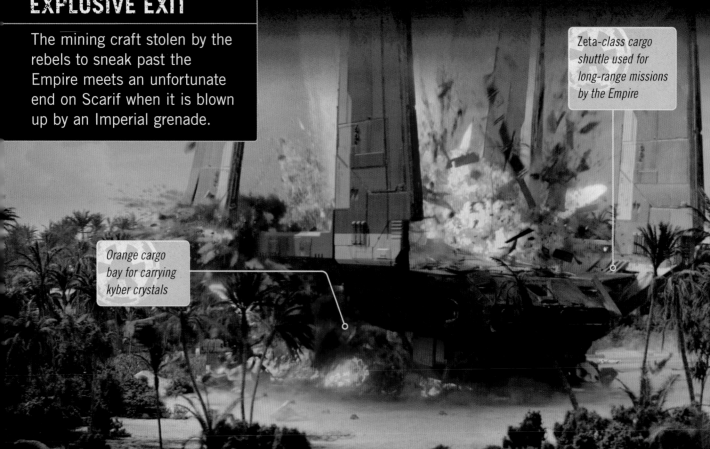

Zeta-class cargo shuttle used for long-range missions by the Empire

Orange cargo bay for carrying kyber crystals

ESCAPING EADU

A heavy military presence greets the rebels on Eadu. Jyn and the team must use cunning and nerve to escape without becoming embroiled in a fight.

BLIND MAN'S BLUFF

On occupied Jedha, wise rebel Chirrut has a different approach to fighting—he senses his enemy's presence before they see him, often taking them by surprise.

KRENNIC COMMANDS

Director Krennic is prepared to use violence to get what he wants. His death troopers are always ready and waiting to carry out his commands.

REBEL FIGHTERS

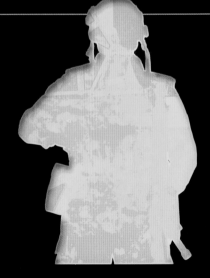

REBEL ROUSERS

Rebel marines are trained to fight. Commandos Bistan and Pao are fierce in battle and are great assets to the Rogue One team.

SEFLA

Lieutenant Sefla leads the rebels on the ground on Scarif. He is camouflaged for sneaking across the jungle and beach terrain.

Y...

The ... at ... whe...
rebel leade... and strategists gathe...
...iant screens and hologr... ...ays
...aps or gathered intelligence.

© LFL

JYN ERSO

LOYALTY

PAO

SLICING SKILLS

Director Krennic

Imperial TIE fighter

BRAVERY

BAZE MALBUS

Scientist
Galen Erso

STEALTH

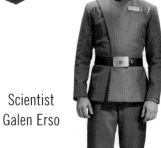

LEADERSHIP

BODHI ROOK

Death Star control room

CASSIAN ANDOR

Imperial
TIE striker

CHIRRUT ÎMWE

UNDERCOVER

BISTAN

INITIATIVE

Imperial
Death Star

A BAND OF ROGUES

K-2SO

DARTH VADER

SCARIF

WEETEEF CYU-BEE

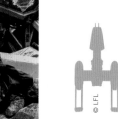

Battlefield Baze

LAH'MU

Jyn on Jedha

KRENNIC'S SHUTTLE

KRENNIC'S GUARDS

HOLY CITY PILGRIM

YAVIN 4

THE DEATH STAR

THE *DEVASTATOR*

EADU

ORSON KRENNIC

IMPERIAL GUARDS

Raddus

Rebel Jyn

MOROFF

KRENNIC'S VISION

JEDHA

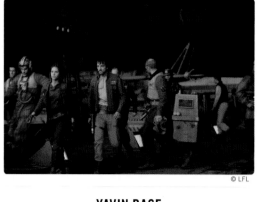

YAVIN BASE

Scarif
shoretrooper

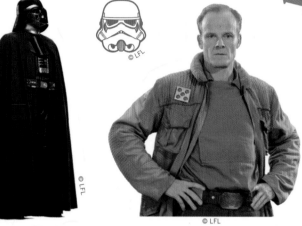

GENERAL DRAVEN

KEEPING SECRETS

Sith Lord

PLAYING SIDES

Stormtrooper on Scarif

Imperial superweapon

GALEN ERSO

MON MOTHMA

TOGNATHIAN SOLDIERS

GENERAL DODONNA

GALEN ERSO'S DAUGHTER

ERSO FAMILY

Rebel
GNK droid

Chirrut

PILOT IN PERIL

SAW GERRERA

Trooper   Battle-ready Pao

GENERAL MERRICK

Imperial
death
trooper

A FATHER'S CALL

DEATH STAR DIRECTOR

CONTROL ROOM

Bowcaster

JYN AND CASSIAN

Rebel droid

Imperial
stormtrooper

BAZE AND CHIRRUT

DEATH STAR GUNNER

DRAVEN'S DOUBTS

DEATH STAR TROOPER

IMPERIAL TRAITOR

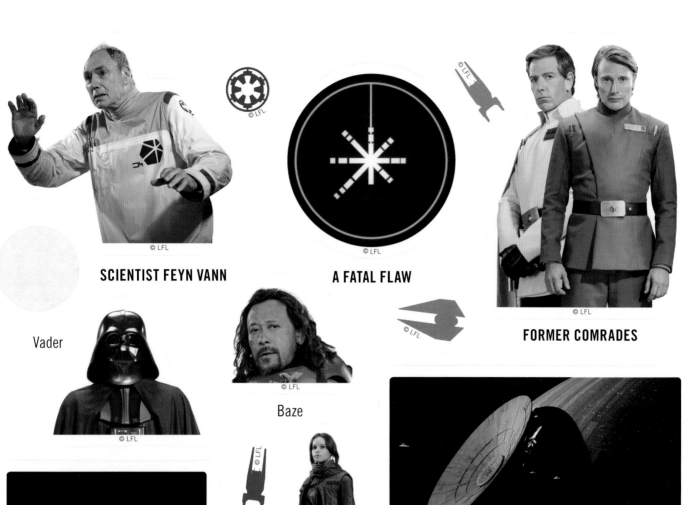

SCIENTIST FEYN VANN

A FATAL FLAW

FORMER COMRADES

Vader

Baze

Jyn

A LOOMING THREAT

FATHER FIGURE

OBEYING ORDERS

REBEL FACTIONS

Warrior monk

X-WING

HARB BINLI

REBEL ROUSERS

HELMET 3

"BLUE FOUR"

AT-ACT ATTACK

PRIVATE KAPPEHL

PRIVATE BASTEREN

HELMET 2

Imperial might

ESCAPING EADU

Y-WING

SCARIF SKY BATTLE

HELMET 1

SCARIF BEACH ASSAULT

U-WING

Cassian

KRENNIC COMMANDS

ZAL DINNES

HEFF TOBBER

Mercenary Moroff

Jyn's father

SEFLA

BLIND MAN'S BLUFF

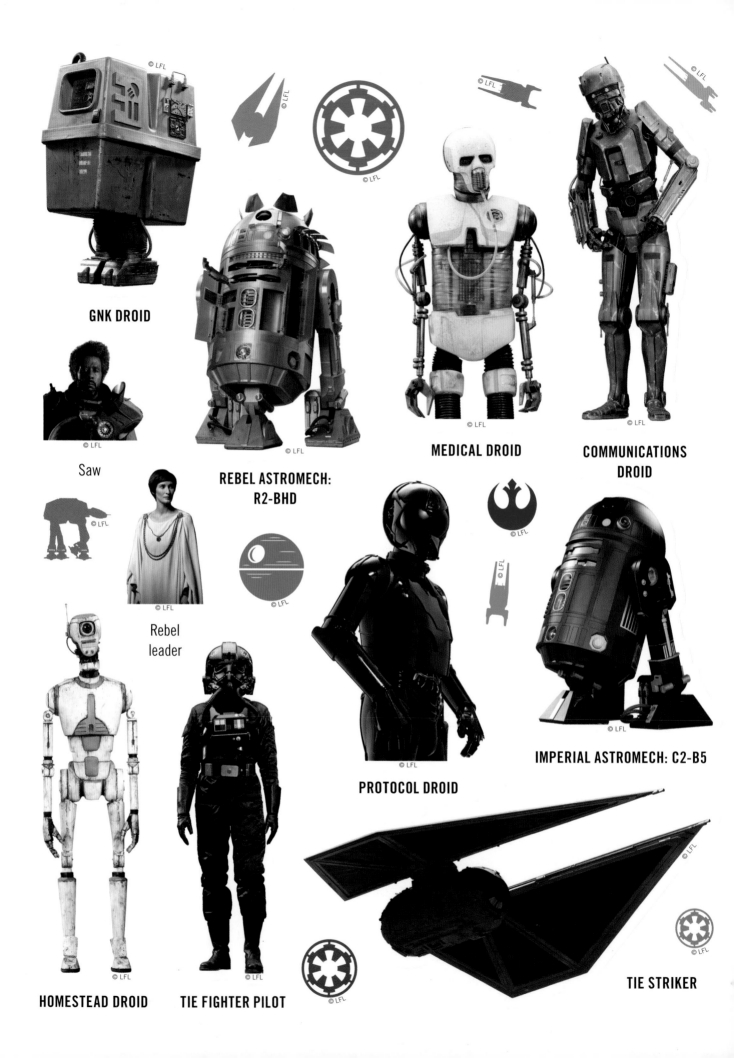

GNK DROID

Saw

REBEL ASTROMECH:
R2-BHD

MEDICAL DROID

COMMUNICATIONS
DROID

Rebel
leader

PROTOCOL DROID

IMPERIAL ASTROMECH: C2-B5

HOMESTEAD DROID

TIE FIGHTER PILOT

TIE STRIKER

TIE FIGHTER

Rebellious rebel

AT-ST

LANDING CREW

Captain Cassian

R3-S1

IMPERIAL TANK

Lyra
Erso

Reprogrammed droid

MOUSE DROID

Lieutenant
Sefla

AT-ACT

ON THE OFFENSIVE

© LFL

STORMTROOPER

© LFL

Emperor's
emissary

© LFL

GUARD DUTY

© LFL

© LFL

© LFL

SHORETROOPER

© LFL

© LFL

© LFL

Yavin 4 control room

© LFL

Death Star plans

© LFL

© LFL

Krennic

© LFL

Rebel Y-wing

© LFL

TANK COMMANDER

© LFL

© LFL

© LFL

TANK TROOPER

© LFL

© LFL

© LFL

DEATH TROOPER

© LFL

Rebel Pao

© LFL

HEAVY ARMOR

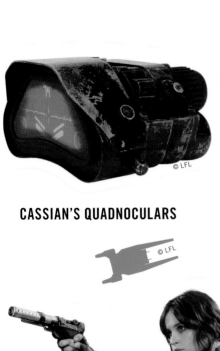

CASSIAN'S QUADNOCULARS

BAZE'S REPEATING BLASTER

UNDERCOVER JYN

Battle-ready Jyn

CHIRRUT'S BOWCASTER

Trooper defense

JYN'S GUN

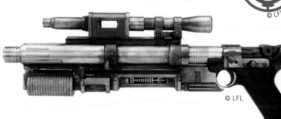

CHIRRUT'S STAFF

Running K-2SO

Rebel Bistan

Rebel X-wing

PREPARED CASSIAN

Rebel Mon Mothma

EXTRA STICKERS

EXTRA STICKERS

EXTRA STICKERS

EXTRA STICKERS

EXTRA STICKERS

© LFL

© LFL

© LFL

© LFL

© LFL

© LFL

© LFL

© LFL

© LFL

© LFL

© LFL

© LFL

© LFL

© LFL

EXTRA STICKERS

© LFL

© LFL

© LFL

© LFL

© LFL

© LFL

© LFL

© LFL

© LFL

© LFL

© LFL

© LFL

© LFL

© LFL

© LFL

© LFL

© LFL

© LFL

© LFL

© LFL

EXTRA STICKERS

© LFL

© LFL

© LFL

© LFL

© LFL

© LFL

© LFL

© LFL

© LFL

© LFL

© LFL

© LFL

© LFL

© LFL

© LFL

© LFL

© LFL

© LFL

© LFL

EXTRA STICKERS

© LFL

EXTRA STICKERS

© LFL

© LFL

© LFL

© LFL

© LFL

© LFL

© LFL

© LFL

© LFL

© LFL

© LFL

© LFL

© LFL

© LFL

© LFL

© LFL

© LFL

© LFL

© LFL

EXTRA STICKERS

EXTRA STICKERS

EXTRA STICKERS

© LFL

© LFL

© LFL

© LFL

© LFL

© LFL

© LFL

© LFL

© LFL

© LFL

© LFL

© LFL

© LFL

© LFL

© LFL

© LFL

© LFL

© LFL

EXTRA STICKERS

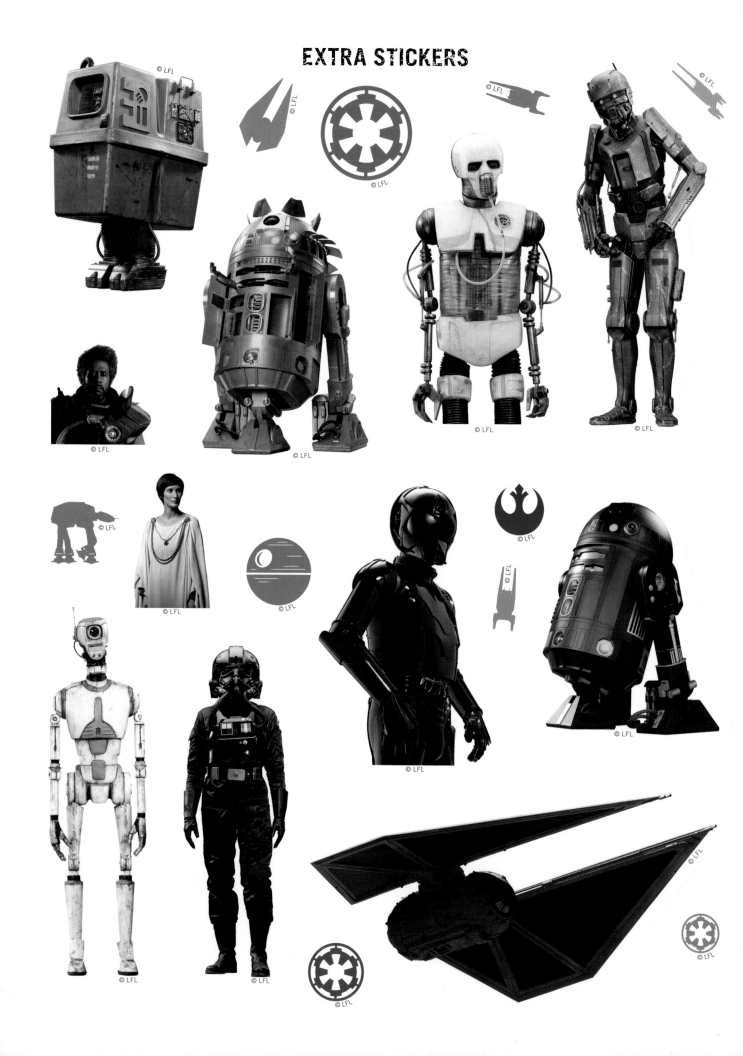

EXTRA STICKERS

EXTRA STICKERS

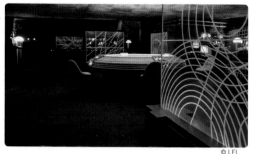

© LFL

EXTRA STICKERS

EXTRA STICKERS

EXTRA STICKERS